Collateral

Collateral

by Gary Lemons

~ 2026 ~

Collateral

Editor-in-chief
Eric Morago

Operations Associate
Shelly Holder

Associate Editors
Mackensi E. Green
Allysa Murray
Rob Sturma
Ellen Webre

Editor Emeritus
Michael Miller

Cover art
Scott Ferry

Book design
Michael Wada

Moon Tide logo design
Abraham Gomez

Collateral
is published by Moon Tide Press

Moon Tide Press
6709 Washington Ave. #9297
Whittier, CA 90608
www.moontidepress.com

FIRST EDITION

Printed in the United States of America

ISBN # 978-1-957799-51-3

für Nöle
Unsere Liebe wird niemals enden

Preface

Collateral in its common usage means to pledge or put up something of value hoping to obtain something of greater value. It might be money—time—materials—family—children—land—often something perhaps irreplaceable. It's a form of gambling—surely—which means no matter the pledge there's an element of desperation and of course the greater the need the greater the desperation. What was pledged is forfeited if things go wrong.

I remember riding my horse at a full gallop toward a jump higher than I'd ever taken—what's forgotten is the moment the exhilaration of making the leap was greater than the fear of falling—and of course the horse has something to say about this as well.

The poems in Collateral aren't blind to the sometimes subtle sometimes graphic suffering that happens as we move from first breath through illness—deprivation— isolation. It's hard to imagine this if we are comfortable with sufficient resources to experience love and happiness and good health but deep in our bodies I believe when other lives suffer we feel it too. Then what—put up our collateral—risk everything to help—think of Doctors Without Borders—or turn our backs and walk away—or—as most of us do—build our house somewhere in between.

These poems—all art I suppose—are vessels with life inside them. The witness and the victim merged. My life as both can be found in these poems. If I'm lucky some of yours may be in them too.

It's important to me to say that the long poems in my books especially in this one are short complete poems designated by 3 starred sections. The sections can be read in any order or they can be read individually or in sequence together as they are presented here. In the same way that most books of poetry are not intended to be read sequentially from first page to last so to in my long poems the reader is invited to see them as images in a gallery—related yet independent consequently initially experienced more through feeling than thought much in the way a painting evokes responses—a composite of brush strokes if you will—each of which in itself stands alone but in composite makes the painting whole.

Contents

Stay out of my valley and let my mountain be.

—Ma Rainey

I am obliged to perform in complete darkness
operations of great delicacy
on myself.

—John Berryman, "Dream Songs No. 67"

Early Lessons

The boy threw a rock at the bird
In the cottonwood tree overhanging the house
Where they both lived—

He threw it hard—intending to kill the bird—
Something primal—deranged —in the genetics of boys.

Let's be precise—it was a goldfinch returned
From a two-hundred-day migration just in time
To become a target singing to the sun.

The rock missed the bird which flew away.

The rock ricocheted off a couple branches
Then hit the boy in the face—the boy carried
The crescent moon scar to his grave—

Make no mistake—I was that boy.
I was that bird.

Without Food

My grandmother made meals of crickets
Learned from her mother—their singing told us where they hid—
We went into the yellow fields at dawn—they sang
Even in our hands—once fried grandmother mashed
Them with a big spoon then served them on soft bread
Made from millet grown in the same fields.

I grew up sharing my early life with family
So it is nothing now to stand in front of rifles
And demand they go back inside the ghosts
That raised them—today the smoke is coming
From distant cities—birds of all sorts perch on our roof
Watching the weathervane disturb black air—
We taste gunpowder on the wind—the birds are silent—
I'm crying even though I'm grown up now—I've lost
So much and don't want to lose any more but the birds
Know better—silence gives the gods no satisfaction—our groans
Make them happy—we are what rifles use for fuel—the cries
Of the people—the silence of the witnesses—when we close
Our eyes does the world get uglier or more beautiful—
Only the living can answer this.

Demonstration

The fish can't get past the dam—
Up or down—they're stuck in old imperatives
And so dissolve slowly back into water—
Into the rocks—the mouths of bear—
Become part of a different world
Where holding still is possible—we learn
From this—one elderly woman puts her walker
On the ground then lifts a banner—the crowd
Gathers—nothing moves except flies in the shallows—
It starts again—batons swing into heads—tear
Gas in the air—people trampled under boots—
The fish throw themselves against the dam
Until battered to death—the impassable this time
Wins—but not always—one day the dams
Will be gone—the once broken people
Will be restored by the waiting that awaits.

Blind Luck

Barbara raised me—my father didn't
Like me calling her mom though I loved
Her more than the fading memory of my own mother
Who walked out when I was 8.

I helped Barbara iron her hair
Using a clear gel that smoked as the tight curls
Straightened —made the house smell
Of acorns popping in a leaf fire.

To this day I think of her looking
At a magazine cover of a white woman with straight
Hair while I brushed out her burnt ends.

I said—how come you do that
When you've got such pretty hair.
She said—I don't know—want to
Look beautiful I guess—I said—
But mom you already do—and she kissed
Me then we sat on the stoop
And watched the neighborhood burn.

The Hood

I know I won't walk
That way ever again but back
Then it was the holy
Street that led past the pet store
Where in a small cage in the window
My future barked
For me to take it home.

Broken Flowers

The baby step is the first and often the last
Time we feel the bones in our bare feet—here
Is the foundation of pumpkins and principles upon
Which a life is built—there is earth underfoot—there are
Victories down there—love—tenderness and cruelty—
Roots of giant trees—broken flowers—this place where
Humanity is bronzed into spirit by the spin of liquid iron—
We are that close to sharing fire and water—the tiger—
Is here—the raptor—great Auk—little Bush Moa—
Grandmothers and children and that dead male bird
Still trying to attract a mate—the land is immune
To the hydraulics of its occupants— we're the mulched
Breath—changelings—mountain into sand washed
Out on the ebb—returned—rebuilt with snow
And forests—wolverines and elk—wildflowers on our spine—
A blue breath in a puff of dark matter come to life
Inside a star as we sleep until far away our light touches
A cradle where music is heard for the first time—the wind dispels
Hung leaves—each child the earth from which the next
Rises—shadows growing heavy—igniting into things
Running out of time—out of space—but never ammunition.

Shifting Ground

A city smokes in the eyes of a boy whose
Mother wipes blood from his hair with her hands—

She's weeping behind ashes through a veil
As the rancid expectorants from furniture
And glass and organics thicken the air
With the seductive promises sung to little
Ones everywhere—tomorrow will be better
Than this—a horse fly lands on the wrist of a soldier—
Where did it come from—why does it bite—
Who built these doors for demons to enter our
Bodies with blueprints that turn devotion
Into an instrument of war—yet—

At the bottom of stairways—in makeshift
Bunkers underground—or dodging thrown stones—
Women are teaching women to read.

***

A hawk stops circling to descend
On a cart pulled by a woman in wooden
Shoes—what is she moving between
Those who have nothing—the women wraps her
Duties tightly around her emptiness to keep it
From spreading—she's a capacitor from which sparks
Escape—defying the gods with her personal fire—
She bites her tongue to make it bleed so when enemy
Soldiers kiss her they'll taste what they've done.

***

No one sings anymore but the children
And their songs are sad—a photographer
With many awards for being where the bodies
Pile up captures another marriage to steel splinters—
Everything here is momentarily virginal—worn
To the bone by the tread of anointed heresies
Come to enable the ancient inaccuracies
That contain so little truth the women that
Learned to read choose not to.

***

Say it to me says the nurse increasing pressure
On a vein—tell me your name—where is my son— mother asks—
The doctor looks away—then crossing his fingers says—
He's safe—right here—beside you.

Gangs

If in your mind you go back
To the old neighborhood
Where the sound of cards flapping
On bicycle spokes backdrops
A skinned knee or racing toward
A finish line not even the passing
Years brings into view
Notice the faces behind curtains
Are unchanged—still old or young—the grass
No shorter or longer—streets wide or narrow or potholed
Still wide or narrow or potholed—the light
Elastic and the sky colored
By the suffering and joys of the lives
Painting it blue from below.

No one who hasn't been
A child knows what it's
Like to love something
That isn't there.

12 Hours

At one o'clock in the morning
I wake up to find my bed unoccupied.

At two in the morning I curse
When one hand of the clock falls off.

At two-thirty in the morning I open my eyes
To become—briefly—worldly.

At three in the morning I hear two rodents
Debating the Man Without Qualities behind the wallpaper.

At four in the morning nothing happens.

At five the neighbor's dog barks
Although I have no neighbors.

At six I try again to sleep—go back to work
Cascading through boulders on the empty page.

At seven I pedal a grindstone
To sharpen numbness into anger.

At eight it's time to shape the poem
Into a sparrow then fling it through the keyhole.

At nine in Alaska above the north pole
A white bear eats the last chip of ice it stands on.

At ten I mistake the train whistle for regulators
Regulating the purring inside a burlap bag.

I hope this is helpful—perhaps we might synchronize
Watches—it will be one in the morning everywhere at once—
The salt marsh will teem with microscopic tissue
Mating in the surging tide while the tear-stained

Pillow tells us how alone we used to be—the old moon is
A barquentine wrecked in the desert—the light the body

Absorbs hurts less than before—it's hot and piercing
As an owl ss the branch beneath it breaks

A Shot of Light Before It Ends

There was a time when my friends
And me were at war with the world which
Means we were at war with ourselves—not
A polite skirmish but a no-win black flag battle
In the trenches with flares and dirt flying
And parts of others in the air we breathed.

We were raggedy teens in wolf packs
Going where we pleased in a narrowing circle
That left us in a sweaty garret inches apart—
And what a sight—braided hemp rope knotted
To keep rowboats from drifting—lank hair—cigarettes—
No where to run—dirty—confused—free.

I wanted this one girl as badly as she wanted me
Though I never saw her again—that's not true—
She lives in my hand—
We collaborate on everything I do—we're bandmates
Rocking one song on separate instruments—we're the one
The many became back when the pain threshold
Seemed like the entrance to a magic theatre—
A place so dark the gleam of a tooth was enough
To see the dice come up snake-eyes —it was bombers on fire
Over enemy terrain and parachutes that sometimes
Worked and landing meant nothing at all—
Time without haste is what we asked of the night.

I read in Ireland the saints ride bees
Between flowers to refresh their souls—
Whatever I just said I don't understand now
But everything was clear then—

I can say a few things about soul if you want—
Myth assigns them to us at birth—so I'm cruising
Roads between farms with friends—drinking and driving
On a hot August far from the gutted cities where our parents
Take pills to stand upright—I throw an empty out the window
But as I let go I see a little boy step out of the woods
Into its path—he might be a cosmic joke or maybe me
Or both but the can hits him in the head—I yell at the driver
To stop then run to the kid and tell him I'm sorry—

Then I got pissed off—ask him what the fuck he's
Doing all by himself out here and where are his parent—me
Self-righteous as a square—kid lights up a cigarette then offers
One to me and we smoke a while—
Said it again—Where's your father kid—
And he blows a smoke ring in my face—eight—maybe
Nine years old dig that and says—I think I just found him—
And that's what I know about soul.

Hitchhike

I remember taking my sister
Piggyback across the swamp because she was afraid
Of snakes and didn't believe me when
I said this is a dream and there's no snakes here—I needed
Her with me—she was all I had of friend
Or family—so I carried her toward that day
When she set me down.

Among these musings a vehicle
Stops and a door opens—I climb in
And we're off—to some great adventure
With no one at the wheel.

How It Begins

The youngest of us—nine—was good
With money—adept at finding the sweetest
Figs for the least sum—mother gave
Her coins to buy a fish for dinner—

Two aunts—their husbands casualties—
Come to share a meal so we ironed tablecloths
And put hibiscus on the windowsills—tradition
Demands hospitality even in times like these—
We celebrate what isn't gone—share the main
Course carved thin enough to go around.

The nine-year-old never returns—
We see plumes of black smoke out the window—
Loud thumps like carpet cleaning day—one aunt
Who isn't deaf yet hears the sirens coming closer—
The explosions are muted like summer
Sunlight in the pockets of a folded dress.

A full glass of water—fire devoid of light—
An empty chair at dinner is only the beginning.

Non-Dualism

A gray bird circles a quaking aspen
During the coldest winter above the Arctic
Circle on record—polar bears watch

Caribou stream across churned snow
Making an endless dark river of instinct and hunger
Circling back to the headwaters of predation
Where the three of us come ashore to
Each pick one thing in this vast world to save.

I pick the gray bird.

You pick the white bear.

The third of us sails away and by
Refusing to choose saves all of us.

Enemies

Peddled only a few blocks
From home one day on my bike
Before running into a crowd of kids
My age with sticks
And rocks just waiting
For a stranger to ride by—

Then the ice cream truck
Turned the corner playing
Circus music—when it stopped
Right across from us a man
In a white uniform jumped out—

I didn't have any money
So the biggest of the strange boys
Bought me a popsicle.

Riding home afterwards
And with all the years to think
Back on it I'm pretty sure
The rocks they threw as I was leaving
Missed me on purpose.

The Host

We spoke from the heart all that summer
On the dock of the small lake between our two houses—
I was 13 and my neighbor 16—she peeled sunburn from her skin—
Tossed it on the water like bait the bluegill snapped up—
I was hypnotized by the shiny new skin on her shoulders—
She told me the fish now knew her—they'd eaten her
Like in church and would live in her forever.

Once I whittled a piece of old cheese into a horse shape—
She nibbled the shavings where mold grew like algae
On the flat-tailed beavers I saw mating in the miner's candles.
I told her she smelled of sunlight—then she kissed me
And I cried because without her I knew I'd die.

The cemetery is darkening when I walk through it
To where she lies. Mother always said she was a good girl—
A little fast—maybe why she never married—
I was away in school but my brother remembered
She returned to the farm too sick to walk—how she lay
Out in the sun and freckled as she burned—a boy
Wakes up a man—snow is coming through an open
Window—when I went to bed it was summer and we
Were young and she was alive—outside a beaver—alone—
Drags trees toward the pond to build its home—
A birch branch in its mouth like a white flag
Held high when soldiers are overrun—sometimes
The world gives up when it seems outnumbered—even on love—
But she never did and I never will.

No Too High Places

Me and Jean snuck in her father's library
Where he kept his medical books on disease
And amputations with color photographs
He used to scare his kids into behaving.

One book though—big as a catcher's mitt—he kept
On a shelf he didn't think we could reach but for the young
There are no too high places.

Here were pictures of soldiers in white tents undergoing
Bloody surgeries by flickering lantern light while outside
The tent flap muddy phantoms stared from holes in the dirt—
In one of the pictures—identified by name—lay Jean's
Grandfather—his hairless white leg on the ground
Beside him with the boot still on it.

In school we read about the war to end all wars.
Maybe it's time to re-write the books.

Meanwhile in a veteran's hospital a nurse
Sutures the raw edges of two conflicting affections—love
And loyalty—doctors extract a bullet from a shattered
Body then slap it until it starts to breathe.

Revolutionaries

The woman is bleeding on the bed—
She tripped over the dog—fell against the dinner
Table—the dog is outside howling—I wipe the floor
Of spilled soup then save the pieces of the bowls
To glue later—my fingers are yellow as nicotine from turmeric—
Father ignores this—he's at war with the government—
Mumbling over a cigar about geography—out the window
The bull uses horns to break down the gate—
Now the bull is on the bed with mother—

I run out into the grass as fast as the bull
Became part of the family—a possible future calls to me
Like a dinner bell awakens a fat uncle—the little
Girl turns to me—we've been together since
Before we were born—one lung each—one
Eye each—sharing the same view—mother
Sets out new bowls—the war goes on—the red days
Don't end here—there's enough of the hen we raised
From an egg left to make another soup—
The bull doesn't care when the candle goes out—
It sees even better in the dark.

Call to Order

In the coverless grimoire held together by faith
And money and the sweaty unguents of despair in an urban
Church filled with hushed worshippers of the bottom line
A corpulent totem pole puffs tobacco hand-rolled inside a $100
Bill while introducing the finance minister who traces
His lineage back to a relative that designed bed pans for King
Midas— the parishoners are green from smoking
Their prayers right down to the butt distracting the speaker
Enough to speak honestly—adjusting his zipper like a cat climbing
A ladder—of his confusion—his nausea—from writing
Motivational speeches without a single word
Of truth—outside the church women gather with nothing
To lose—they are now inside the speaker's worse
Nightmare where they cut the umbilicus between the theft
Of today and the fear of unrestrained equality
With garden shears last used
To behead a fragrant rose.

Busker

The guitar player on the corner
Picking out an old blues song
Doesn't care about the history
Of pain and sorrow—she wants to stop
Hurting long enough to play a waltz—
Buskers on every corner share her desire
For a warm bed but settle for yawning parents
Pushing shy children from safety to put a dollar
In the guitar case—she grows old as the centuries pass
And dies on the pavement beneath a neon
Sign sparkling on the snow trapped in her dyed
Red hair—she's Irish and grown old but vain
Enough at the end to pray the wee folk
Touch her gently when they come.

I don't remember the lyrics to her song
But I know that I loved her brave contralto
Adrift in the frozen air—I gave her my
Coat and all the love I could spare—we
All come to the realization that small
Acts of mercy are sometimes not enough.

Interregnum

The odd duck in the dormitory
Received a wedgie the first time he aced
Four tests in one day then posted
The results outside his door.

The dunderheads who broke into
His room to steal his secrets found nothing
They understood—left without knowing the boy
Swabbed cayenne pepper on the doorknob
Until they rubbed sleep from their eyes.

Twenty years later the gulf
Between the tormented and tormentor
Is so wide a comet streaks through it
Without touching either side and though
Dinosaurs boiled inside their skins the redwoods
Flourished in the steam

Disease and Medicine

The few things we see are falling apart—
In cities—in suburbs—rural areas—beneath the freeway
Lives are lit up then put out—breath is only seen when it's
Cold—it's always cold somewhere—how do we know
We're alive—days are a work of art where decay curates
Longevity—I feel ill—help me—where is the medicine
For this disease—outside the circus tent people
Pay admission to come inside to see someone in a cage
That can't stop laughing——I wouldn't want to see that—
All structures have unseen interiors—-my grandmother's quilting
Room had mice—I have breath I can't see except in winter.

Behind the deli counter—gentle hands butcher
A goose in a copper sink prior to a holiday—ever mindful
Of profit feathers are sold to a pillow factory after the liver
Is made into pâté—for connoisseurs of last moments please
Take notice when the interior of the butcher
And the goose are forever the same—

In death the goose—like my father—becomes an ocean
Undercutting coastal houses—drawing them outward
On rising waves—the celebrants inside—gorged—
Are sick to their stomachs—the house is in heavy seas—
The tide is (always) going out—acknowledging what's wrong
Is the only instrument in the recidivist's quartet—

The last saint jumps out the window into the sea
Then paddles toward sunset on a bit of broken wood
That was once a closed door—she's erasing feathers and long held
Convictions from her eulogy—the hissing we hear is the ocean
Cascading over the flat earth to who knows where—

The sun is a teapot—I didn't mention the saint is a vegetarian
And that her paddles are celery stalks—all thoughts of normalcy
Left with the circus—the happy man is pouring tea
That will be cool enough to drink when this poem
Is done— the medicine works— have a sip—every single
Life you save from here on out is your own

Ink

for Kelly and Georgia and Greg and John

In the upstairs print room there are seven dinosaurs—5
Working Chandler & Price letter presses— two more for parts
As well as my thrift shop mattress in one corner on the floor
Beside the drip-coffee maker that gives the room a mixture of burnt
Beans over sour ink—a smell I loved then and fifty years later love
Even more because it brings its incandescent light——Vermont
Winters—lubricious ghosts and poetry—the smell of changes
Sweet and wet and gaunt animals without a home—

So we cared for them—the shy ones that step from the forest
Lit up by roadside flares—promiscuous angels that desire
Supple appendages —chaste ones that never leave your side—
Listening to every word—some too thin to move—some too heavy
To fly—all of them beloved hieroglyphs peeled like fried
Chicken down to the meat then fed to the press at midnight.

We are learning to cry—it's enough we lived and loved
Without restraint—loved without shame in the old way of intaglio-
Stamped into one another—bound bone to spirit—
The text growing brighter as the ink fades.

October Sky

We rescued the thoroughbred that Spring—
An old racehorse that never won headed for the dogfood bowl—

The pastures drain snow by design so we put her out
Six hours a day with her stablemate—a pygmy goat—after a few
Days they were inseparable—touching noses under the big
Elm beginning to fill winter branches with sighing leaves.

We cleaned her hooves—brushed her chestnut coat—
Wormed her—made sure she knew this was her forever home—
Soothing each bad twitch one at a time—letting her
See love is that hand without a whip.

By fall she knows she's safe. The elm in the pasture
Begins to drop its green dreams—she stands beneath
Them as they fall on her—she lets them—like a soft brush
I imagine—she pushes her face into me when I
Lift her hooves to pick out the packed dirt
In her frogs. I buried her a decade later in Autumn
As a cold wind stripped the elm bare—two barn
Cats watched from the porch in a slant of yellow dust—
Her name was and is Rosy—it gets louder doesn't it—
The light that calls us home.

Crack the Whip

Kids join hands in a long chain with a big boy
At the head and the smallest at the tail—

Then the big boy pulled the chain—slowly at first—
Across the playground—through the windows
Of memory there's a blue sky with the metallic
Smell of rain far off or maybe it's coming out of the soil
As if an iron flower went to seed—there's birds overhead—
Bob Whites in the fields calling their children home—

The whip moves faster—kids tripping on each other
To keep from letting go—the momentum builds—eccentric
Half circles with fast changes in directions
Until the end of the whip—the smallest child—
Can't hold on—lets go and is forever gone.

I hear the Bob White calling—follow this sound
As far as living allows—out to where all songs jumble
Into the lullaby angels hear before the gods teach
Them how to love what they can't save.

Second Chances

I drag the face with its brave smile
On a litter into the triage tent for those
In need of a transplant—their injuries
So mortal death seems the best way out—
So much more work to be done—if you believe this
Then carry the skin back to the ostrich
Made into boots—the spilled pollen from cut flowers
Back to the garden for the bees
That mourn not the loss of beauty
But how much we charge it—

The willing carry the weight
No one else will—describe it with every
Step before setting it down—here—
On this child I unburden my father—on this
One my mother—or am I the sum of those
That know everything of duty but
So little of joy they never say their names
Out loud to the falling rain.

Manassas

He's a tree on a prairie but throws
No shade—is perhaps the shade itself—he has
No reference other than his shadow changing all day
Until night swallows them both—his bark is dark
Gray—the color of gun smoke coagulated
On the ground after it rains—her bonnet
Has red holes in it—she backstrokes
In the heartwood—surges into the highest
Leaves then brings back heat like a steamship's
Double defecator leaks fuel in the bilge—they are one thing—nurse—
Patient—tree—they plant a flag among the swirling
Hours—watch the soldiers still fighting taken in mid-stride
Then re-taken to the pastures of the open wound—
They love more than humanely possible way down
In the roots—winter leaves no prisoners above ground—

They are one thing—always were though late
To this understanding—home for birds and birdsongs—come
Spring the prairie turns white with flowers
From which they look out at death
And renewal with wet lips and dry eyes.

Missing in Action

It happens so slowly,
A small bare vine planted
In spring become a trellis bent
By summer flowers—

Mother details something sewn
With intricate stitches on a couch
Beside father, watching television,
Both flickering and silent.

Father goes into the garage
To check on some noise he thinks
Might be mice and never comes out.
Mother sets down her needlepoint,
Walks to a closet for more yarn. Never
Returns. Brothers go out into sunlight and
Birdsongs, disappear into the years.

I wait for it all to return.
Wait in the darkness without breath
Listening to a million hearts, none
Of which are mine, beating.

Veterans

In a field of golden tansy
Beside the creek called Bull Run
Crabapples hang like targets in hot air—we sight
Along a finger—shoot them and never miss—imagine
We're the branches shaped by resistance
To winds that couldn't break them.

Union veterans say surgeons threw
Arms and legs in that little creek as the battle
Raged further north knowing the body parts
Would drift downstream where the rebels
Watered horse and filled their canteens.

Today which is always yesterday my brother
And I fish the creek for Crappie and Rock Bass—
This particular morning the fog hides the tops
Of the trees. When the crabapples fall
They taste bitter as a tuning fork—like a thing
That never cries—like the gun my brother
Tasted just before he died.

At Sea

With our backs to the derelict freighter
We pass through stages of admiring so much
Natural beauty into silently becoming one
With it—the rusted old hulk leaves blood
Where we touch it but who doesn't leave
Blood behind them—it's what people do—even
The best pollinate dripping red flowers—
The gray sea slides through pink toward blue
Like a Miles Davis solo—on the ebb we touch
Precious reminders—opalescent shells softening
Into sand dollars—iodine pincher of crabs
Gulls pick apart in reptilian fury—

One of us wonders out loud if raw
Appetite isn't also beautiful.

In this vastness the embroidered threads
Of fishing line wrap a skeletal seal—pull tabs
Festoon its skull—perhaps Zen masters
Might say this too is beauty but our
Bodies revolt—I let go of your hand—
Turn inland where the illusion prevails
But you snatch my hand right back
And say hold on—we're part of this.

In a tidepool of stranded sea stars
A fish flops like one hand clapping—
I want to return it to the waterline but again
You say—no—please leave it—it's been
Here before—your kindness will kill it.

I remember this day vividly
Because even though you're dead now
I keep your compass in my pocket—feel
The salty crystals of your morning breath
On my lips—I throb with secret longing for you
Which is all that keeps me alive...

This wreck might be our grandmother—
The midnight hour her only cargo now—half buried in the dharma
Of the evermore—her purpose renewed as we step
Onboard—the next voyage without destination—
More moments to wander if only the sea brings you back.

Rise and Shine

Sleeping poorly atop a soiled
Pillow a grown man dreams of childhood—
The curtains burning—mother
Pulling me out of bed.

The neighbor girl was an arsonist.
She lit matches in secret places—
Her face flickered between anger and joy
Before settling into the blank expression
Of a canal filled with bullheads
Covered over by green slime. I remember
Her hands were ice cold—

A sunlit shaft of yellow dust blown
Out of forgetfulness through an open window
Into the eyes of crows hopping on one leg—
A tramp in the corn rising behind a tractor
With tire tracks across his back—

And I remember on the playgrounds
Of America the swings moving higher
And higher toward the sun
With nobody on them.

Empathy

I was 9 then.
A hot summer day after
Delivering The Washington Post to 75 homes
On my bike—I walked through fallen
Pink Mimosa flowers smelling honey
Over the wild garlic by the shed.

Into the bath all hot and sweaty
Where I floated my little collection of toys—
Ducks with bright yellow bills—
Frogmen with tridents from a mail-in
Cereal coupon and my favorite—
A baking soda powered boat.

Later in High School gym class
Our white-haired teacher told us
Only disgusting boys take baths—
That it was an offense against nature
To sit in the same water with your asshole.
Made me wonder about his funky laundry basket.
I'm in the tub right now dictating this poem
To my phone as I push the little ducks around
With my toes and feel something difficult to explain
Flow out of my heart as if a river otter crawled
Up my leg to find its way to the sea—
It funny to say but the otter
Reminds me no matter how small our steps
We learn to live more fully moving deeper
Into one another and not away.

Longing for the Past

In the rearview mirror the dead
Party on—holding up a photo of me
As a younger man simultaneously
Throwing confetti while playing
Spin the bottle with a prom queen
Who thinks she should drive.

This is why I rear-ended the school
Bus officer—I'm just glad no one got hurt
Except the prom queen who—being a ghost
And already dead—was barely damaged.

This got me a sobriety test
Which I passed with flying colors—
An expression that comes from a man-of-war
Bearing down on an East Indiaman
To re-steal the spice in its hold.

I lay in the rubble waiting for guidance—
Someone to tell me when it's time to draw
The line in time to step over it—-the party ends
When the police siren gets so loud I decide—realizing
I can't outrun myself—to face the music
For damages I caused with or without intent.

Memory Care

Mother sits in the same chair
Day after day whispering the same thing
To invisible people she calls doctor
Or nurse or father—she's a happy child
Marveling over the inside of an orange for the first time—
Puzzled by her own extremities—asking-
Of illness—why are you so mean—

What mom—what do you see?

And she smiles the way lipstick
Smiles inside its tube—says—snow—
A trembling hand pointing to a setting sun—
Falling snow—it covers everything—
The path ahead—the one behind—
This chair where no one sits.

Blistering Disquietude

No one should become a factory for useless things—
No one need recycle words from the encrusted
Tongues of dead mimes—I walk into a bank with the horn
Of plenty trying to blow it like Miles Davis did.
I soon learn that some deposits can't be withdrawn.

Out of one world as a child into another—
Push back my hair with fingers pointed and yellow as pencils.
Think—I'm alive—something good might happen any minute.

Any place can be a place where it's possible to choose
A new direction—right now I stop and sit down—hold out a cup
Then recite the poems of Adrianne Kalfopoulou and Susan Tepper
To encourage sidewalk passengers to question themselves
As poets do—to unveil the machine gun beneath the estuary—
Where storks mate in the mud—a student of Sappho might
Produce a feminist interpretation of the Yoga Sutras—
When doves are in the air the traffic stops—

From the beauty salon men step out—their dyed
Aigrets wilting in the hot air—leaving a trail of apologies
Behind them—a stranger watching this flings her empty
Bowl on the pavement then says to the men—please
Summarize the things you didn't steal you didn't steal from the storks.
For their feathers—there's a vat of purple dye dried
To the color of a crusader's lustful eye—the warriors
Are poorly oiled relics squeaking like dog toys—

Somewhere in a pasture the storks perch
On the backs of beautiful cattle picking fleas—the men
Lost their voice—they have no words—the women
In the silence thanks them for listening—
The cattle have licked all the mud off the storks—
Everything is clean and speechless once again
In this dwelling of perfect symmetries..

Kaleidoscope

I search for the right words in the tangled
Underbrush near the playground to describe children
Of different ages covered with insect bites
Threatening passengers on a bus briefly idling
Outside the fence where one child pushes another
Down—the passengers breathe the blue exhaust until
The bus takes off into indifferent exile.

I want the children to grow old enough to believe
Kindness is a game with no losers but they need to hear
This at home and in class and not from an invisible
Poet whose voice can be scary but they go about
Their business silently as if everything they say
Helps hasten a disappearance like a ghost
Drowning in a lake leaves no body.

It's okay that no one is a child forever.

Bodhisattva

The witches fly in the rain
Above sweating mangrove bays—
Through wildfire smoke —through
Shuttered houses while everyone sleeps—
Through children thrown overboard
From a ship of fools—through all
Events—real and imagined—
Through each human—the
Living or deadly door into
An empty bowl of blood
And fragile augury
Where death like
Life is a place
Of solemn
Wonder.

Villanelle

Those who want to find me know where to go.
They can walk through green tunnels in the rain;
Covering the path so no one follows.

Some stumble naked through the frozen snow
Or sleep in warm patches where deer have lain.
Those who want to find me know where to go.

So many things we love but few will know
In any season what they lost or gained
Covering the path so no one follows

Them into the young corn while the scarecrow
Sleeps beneath a sky filled with inkblot stains.
Those who want to find me know where to go.

The suffering child needs the light to grow;
The dark to point the way forward again
Covering the path so no one follows.

Stand together where waters ebb and flow.
Sing loudly your song but softly your name.
Those who want to find me know where to go
Covering the path so no one follows.

Lion Country

Snorkel the waste stream of the villanelle—job interviews
For the somnambulist smuggling heroes in combustible
Suitcases back and forth between mythologies—thrown
Away lives—words—zoological sketches children fear—
Look in yourself for the world without suffering—
It's in the pink eyes of rabbits—staining the surgeon's
Wet glove—aligns with the tired spring inside
The ballpoint pen—these places the villanelle is extracted
Cautiously like sulfuric acid from a mason jar—-
Searching for truth—not knowing where to begin
But brave enough to begin—climb to the top
Rung of every ladder placed against a burning building
To save the fire from the fire because this is the first
Requirement of the villanelle—the fiefdom where
Yesterday's tear-soaked rags once used to wipe sweat
From piano keys combusts into rhapsody.

***

It's necessary to free the captive swans
In my lover's elegant black dress—the one she wore
When we sambaed on the balcony above the café
Where a concertina player fed his monkey small
Bits of banana-flavored tunes—it's Paris in the villanelle
But autumn in Athens and she is dripping wet after
Falling in the canal—no—that was Venice—
In Athens we fell into a mud puddle disturbing mosquitos—
The one you slapped left blood on your thigh—or maybe that
Was my lipstick—it's hard to spit out spiders while employed
By memory as sunshine in a breathless grove of empty chairs—
Roses lose their beautiful petals but few speak
Speak of how the oboist flung off his toupee.

***

The voice of experience is often mistaken as tinnitus
That when decoded is a dead ancestor cursing
The gosling chasing the honor guard away
From the dictator's tomb—how with our last breath
We blow clarinets in the dark—licking our lips
Then pressing them against the same worn reed
Handed down by elders—taking turns making music—
No longer alone—no longer dying—saved by music—
It was a strange meridian we crossed to arrive here hungry—
Rewarded for our efforts by a rodent that shared
Its stash of cheese—oh for a glass of grigio in crushed ice.

***

Summer storms blow small vessels filled
With refugees from antagonisms—they sail into the marina—
Destinies smuggled inside overt disguises—the captain's tongue
Is stuck in the bung hole of a keg of salted beef—he's seeking
Knowledge to share with the cook with the French accent
Teaching the harbor master new ways to say ahoy—
For all I know those diving birds splashing in the waves
Covet the ink squid squirt on poets spearfishing for their muse.
At any rate—as they say in France—*ohé du navire.*

***

We nearly drowned in the deltas beneath
Belly buttons—rescued by Scottish pipers licking haggis
From each other's kilt on those streets where
The faint echoes of horns awaken local gods asleep
In their privies—regardless of the latitudes of pain
Or the anorectic filament in street corner lamps—
Smell of fish in drains—the smell of fish on the hoofs
Of carriage horses or whiskers of grooms—everything
Kissing everything turns on the milking machine
Attached to a cow with sad eyes.

***

I grasp years later what you meant telling
Me whatever I know is not enough.

***

The poem won't say anything that isn't true.
You and I worked our way across the ocean
Without a boat—we know the place where the collarbone
Dips to catch the rain—we throw stones at suicide
Bombers then stop—they are family too though
More committed to the difficulties of ending the villanelle—
I'll say it now—the edge of the cliff is near—
The drop-off clearly fatal—the view magnetic—
Inside the villanelle Jonah hangs a wreath of holly
On the tube out of the whale—are we granted a last wish—
Mine is to find you in your garden blooming all winter
And taste your fragrance through the slanting snow—
You clap your hands and the bullets are diverted—

We start this and every journey between obliquities
To find solace in each other's arms—the blue
Beech with the gutted stag dripping from a stout limb
Is less guilty by moonlight—in the past we'd see this
And return to the bed to rewrite the poem our lives make
Each time we refuse to look away—but now that darkness
Has settled to the bottom of the glass leaving a sweet blue
Clarity in which we place our tongues—you speak to the tree—
I speak to the stag—we both care about the blood
That drips shiny note by note down from the cut throat to fertilize
The music heard only when the end is near.

Islands

The birds of summer fly away
When leaves start falling—the owls
Drop feathers but stay—
Winter is an old friend chipping summer
Off frozen windowpanes—solidarity
Is the only consolation for standing your ground—
I'm here with them—making snow angels
While reciting a posthumous poem by Robert
Frost who died before finishing
The Wall Between Appearances.

How it is that a warm breeze
Carries the strong scent of a mare foaling
Beneath a chestnut tree—I guess in this life
One should expect when darting between the aisles
In somatic libraries to hear-fi-fi-fo-fum
Coming from the shelves—I do—when
The branch breaks from the strain of my
Added weight I fly away catching no more
Than a glimpse of two oligarchs with no hands
Struggling to flip the hourglass over
Before time runs out.

Dreams Are Dumpsters

How about we start at the ending we want
And work backwards to rewrite a beginning we despise—

The hard part is overlooking the details along the way—
The subway—what the hell—blind moles mating with architects
In underground laboratories for evolution—rats and humans—I
Bet on the rats those whiskery rubbish filters—I once worked in a deli
On Dupont Circle making sausage—replaced a guy that backed
Into the grinding machine—he got a little behind in his work—
No one told the customers until a few sandwiches sold—
There were two delis side by side—we shared and dumpsters—
During smoke breaks I watched the ends of the alley in case
Hope came staggering out of the light drunk enough to be frisked—

That night in a tavern a pilgrim walks toward me—I wish
It ended differently but this is a lost planet with sawdust
On the floor and someone shouting—last call—drink
Up—I turned to you and we kissed like anteaters—a kiss
That hasn't stopped yet—cigarette and chianti taste in the mouth—
A thing like survival rattles trash cans in the alley—looking
For scraps—there's always a thing outside our lives wanting back in—
Making something sacred from what we throw away.

Pilot

I lay half in the mud on my back
In the summer sun with my feet in the water
Of the glacier-fed lake and wiggle my toes
Knowing the ripples startle the ducks
On the other side—perhaps everything on the other
Side will know I'm here—my dead
Mother or brother—saying—ah—he's
Thinking of us again—

Overhead I hear a plane droning like a shruti
Box—it leaves white vapor trails in the pomposity of a perfect sky—

I wonder who flies that plane. I
Wonder if anyone does. Then it's gone.

I close my eyes to awaken a half century
Later from narcotic dreams beneath buzzing lamps
In a hospital bed attached to machines that think
They know my name—that sound again—like something
Once faraway on its final approach.

Stripping With Jesus

Never taken my clothes off in front
Of a savior but once the music started
It was impossible to stop—especially when Jesus
Threw off his robe then whirled his—well—
Sorry to say this—dirty thong across the cave
At which point we began to boogie—never
Touching—to the beat of two hearts
Momentarily become one.

Once naked the movements grew more furious—
Rivers converge at flood stage—Jesus wept seeing
My scars—I wept seeing his—livid rose
Petals plastered on a windowpane—

When the music stopped we got shy—we dressed
Then Jesus pushed the rock away—god he was strong—
A crowd cheered as we stepped out of the dark though we agreed
It felt strange wearing each other's clothes—

Later I heard he wrote a book about what happened—
I did too but mine ends differently

Great great-grandmother

In the overgrown cave under the banks
Of a seasonal creek below ancient oaks in a wilderness
Only a few tramps have seen since the natives
Were murdered here black flies hover above rotting
Acorns—there's grunting from a badger's hole—
I sit with my great-great-grandmother
On my lap as the cave whispers old stories.

There's a harpsichord in her brown hands—
The cave plays it beautifully—my great-great grandmother sings
Me to sleep—songs from her grandmother
And all the mothers before her—
All around me—leaves are blowing—
It must be autumn—

There will never be a time
When listening is not enough.

Smiling At the Shark

I nodded out from exhaustion
And woke up when the needle
Fell from my hand to the floor—

I tried to go straight
But not today so I
Pick up the needle
And return to knitting
The life jacket that one
Day will hopefully save me
From myself.

Beyond Winter

The dandelions don't know they're weeds
So their blues songs are not about loss—their sadness
Comes from devotion to a fickle light—

Where the fence meets the barb wire
A horse leans over but can't reach the piano
Player who—yes—is me—offering salvation songs to a yellow flower—
A baby bird falls from its nest—somersaulting—a naked
Defenseless thing about to arrive—we are this
Or that or them with a teaspoon of rain to give
Our mother dying of thirst.

The elephant lifts its trunk from the river
Then sprays the river on itself—cooling off as the sun
Gets hotter—then sprays more river on creatures
Dying of heat—gives notional swans in Ireland
A chance to disappear into the cool fog above the lake
Where young poets never tire of comparing swans
To fathers sent to war—the dandelions now flower at the end
Of the wrist of the pianist—the horse explains in an impromptu rap
That both sides of the fence divide the same music—

In the ruins of the day a matador teases
Bees by flapping red rose petals like a cape—this
Maddens the hummingbird until the gods
Of war tire of examining one another's scrotums
For heresies that once discovered partition incoherent frenzy
Into ordered clots of poppies on battlefields thereby
Assuring nations there will be no shortages
Of remarkable endings when death is a starter pistol.

This is our journey—not unlike an elephant
Too beautiful to imagine wading into a tiny
Puddle to disappear forever.

Plover Song

Rilke dances between snowflakes afraid of freezing
His fingers off into an overheated room to pluck a tail
Feather from the raven that lives with him to write down
The bird's guidance which crudely stated is—

Schnee bedeckt die roten Seiten.

***

An elderly bone in a hooded robe takes
The cold air treatment for the tubercular
On the porch of a ruined mansion —its double
Circles overhead with a rabbit dribbling sputum from its
Mouth—a corsage of sorts pinned to the idea
Wellness originates between the horns of a musk
Ox struggling toward the northern lights through
A frozen cemetery for cliches—the ox knows you
Hate it and so walks into your poem and shits
Forcing you to strike a bargain with the monkey
Swinging from kiss to kiss inside the shrinking
Jungle of nominal self-restraint.

***

A poem might come from the struggles of dead
Sherpas reborn as ice sculptures ladled
From a stew of granite into a sutra to appease Kali
Who reminds us to be kind to the thing
That did the thing it did.

The man relies perhaps too much on stillness
Between atrocities to help him unhinge
The light from his eyes to give back flame
To the taper he snuffed—the sparrow
In his hand—the spoonful of honey—the ka-ching
Of cash registers underground—these mountains
Where Sherpas take us up but not down.

***

I am becoming dew on the fractal
Of generosity—she is the last woman standing—
We are searching the night sky for the star
That will lead to a house filled with dreams
That work overtime to come true—we understand
It's the effort not the results that matter—
In the garden my father's ghost prunes the white
Roses which—if gone wild—constipate him.

One thing no one can take credit for—
The courage of the civilian packing two sturdy
Boots swapped periodically to help the only foot
Keep walking—she—yes—-carries a black crayon

To draw barns where there are none to shelter
The newborn piglets nursing on the empty page.

***

A grove of ripe oranges—the replacement
Of furniture after painting the room—
So many incidentals confirm the lines of force
Between savants and imbeciles—

Because I am still alive this man
Takes off his watch in the charred baptistery
So as not to place a time limit on how
Many puffs from hookahs demons
Take before perfecting Latin monologues—

A cigar is only a cigar if you call it that—it might
Be a fuse depending on what happens next inside
The limousine slowing down in time for something
To be throw in or out a tinted window—

Rilke's in back—not sure when to ask the driver
To pull over so he can die again—there he says—next
To that swamp where my only true love sits
Atop a toadstool fondling my substitute—

She is done renting out her heart
To poets and shouts over the spring peepers—
You are one lifetime behind on rent.

***

Skuas circle overhead with the remains
Of televangelists broken on rocks in their gullet—
The hairspray and psychobabble disturb
Their digestion—the poet is nearly so involved
In this very real moment that in empathy
He might grow a beak making it hard
To do anything with the truth except peck
Holes in it to be filled later by living.

***

A hymn sung acapella then corked
Into a green bottle bubbles to the surface
Of a mill pond—this is the moment
I remember I'm not only the plover circling
A tragedy beneath funnel clouds but also
Every man and every woman standing
Inside this poem with an umbrella
Hoping not to get wet.

***

Inside a cottage a troubled adolescent
Paints a stick figure of the man he'll become—
Details to be filled in later—the brush sobs
Violet streaks on stretched canvas—sunsets
Caught in a wishing well around which baboons
Switch hands to cover their gleaming parts—

His nanny comes out of a bathroom
In the future with a rat by the tail
And that's when the light bulb explodes.

***

A child that once was me eructates
An enormous dinosaur that coughs out
His parents who cough out Rilke's ghost
That saves this poem from the endless
Formalities of starting over by reanimating
A rickety bridge by crossing it.

What we know is nothing compared to Emily
Dickinson climbing the ladder out of a stagnant pond
Up to the window behind which a featherless bird
Conjures sorrow and hope from its dismal confinement—
Straw into gold—these transformations we learn to love
Or despise before we have a name for them.

Disarming

The dance doesn't end when the bullets
Penetrate the walls nor does the band
Stop covering songs from previous generations
But the sleeve of your blue dress puffs out
As one flying note passes through the fabric
While the bass player jumps on the shooter
And wrestled the gun away—it's not clear
If they marginally changed instruments.

The music travels different octaves
As we hold each other close as bound pages—
The singer steps to the microphone to advise
Everyone it's time for a slow dance—

The band members are parents as well
As musicians—the guitar player retunes
Her instrument to the key of long-stemmed
Roses before cutting one— a spreading lake
Of crimson flowers signifies one dance ended
But unless someone shuts off the power
Another one will soon begin.

Legacy

Nowadays every intimacy is inspected
For inauthenticity by launching a burning paper
Boat from the hips that shoots the rapids
Downstream to the clenched toes before
Sinking inside the spoken word

Alerting the villagers waiting for a sign—
Or street corner preachers chugging
A god—or the paramours grunting
Wet verbs into hearing aids—deliveries
Never scripted that freeze in mid-sentence
Having recognized the reaper in the audience—

Yes we witnessed terrible things—
Atrocious presumptions in the dancehall jingo
Of crows pecking a blister—still we keep going—
Our brain overrides the spirit and steals a car
Then takes us on a joyride on the long
Way home where the vacuum bags
Are filled with dirt from the playroom where
Children—hoping to make it through
Another day—watch their parents juggle
Fatal objects while trying not to cry.

After Everything Is Said

The deaf soldier accidently shot her wife
While loading the squirrel gun on the porch but didn't know
She did—her wife was out in the yard hanging suet
For warblers—they both survived —while hunting for morels along
The river they found two children tied to a cottonwood
Stump so adopted them—home was an island
In the lap of a bright blue goddess that shared her breath
Straight into their mouths—storms blew trees down—
Creeks were damned for drawing water—crickets
Invaded the pantry while red ants traversed the sweaty
Inner thighs of the mule—the work never stopped—
Often they both wished the shot killed someone to disrupt
A numbing routine—but accidents like miracles
Seldom happen when you wish for them.

I read this poem and wonder why I didn't tell
You sooner—didn't warn you before the window slammed
Down on your hand as you reached to pick a red rose—
I am in every way yours—my apron pockets are
Filled with fresh spearmint for making jelly—when
I come back inside to wash my fingernails you are washing
Your hands so we wash each other up to the wrist then go
Into the bedroom take off our clothes and sleep
Awhile as our bodies cool down—when it's nearly

Night you open the family album with clean hands—
There are so few photos of us before the gun went off—

We're both old and deaf now—scarred from potshots
The world didn't even aim—and this is what
I hate to tell you so I'll linger awhile in a silence
So deep it shames the stars—in that special dark—not
One daylit hour left—so close we're one body—
Neighbors hear the gun go off again—
Twice.

Baudelaire Barks

A terrier named Whoopie watches
An elderly man push a wheelbarrow filled with poems
Out into a field where a miniature ziggurat
Is partially completed—the man stops every few
Steps to scratch himself—the dog sees this but looks
Away with envy or perhaps distaste.

The man is always hungry—it's hard work
Filling the dog's bowl—taking care to cause no
Harm—it's work to step carefully—to remember
What plants need watering—to remember names—
The man writes it all down—the little dog approves—
Tails are wagged—the ziggurat grows taller—

Without dogs there would be no poetry.

Ecology of Need

The litmus test for loyalty
Is trusting an ancient scribe with no prophet
In sight writing down the words
Passed on from mother to mother
Like a kiss in which the tongue
Has a subservient role…

Warning sounds distort the silence
Like trip wire set off by missionaries
Attempting to convert wild elephants
Into disciples of Gabriels's horn—

Ignorance is more powerful than
A shovel—like a hammer it's capable
Of getting the wrong job done
At exactly the right time.

In the orchard at the end
Of the picking season one perfect fruit
Still hang—eat it before it falls
Into the wrong hands.

Lighting Candles

Offshore the tanker lists heavily to starboard—
Clinometer readings off the charts—muscular green
Humpbacked waves push it further over exposing
Side thrusters and the cook's butt wedged in a porthole—
This is no way to abandon ship—threads of stinking
Black diesel move into rookeries on the beach.

Holding one cormorant in your hand
So covered with oil you can't see
Its eyes is enough to make you fear
Your potential and slow to welcome the monastic
Tradition of letting anger go—I confess
To Poseidon I envy his trident—there
Are sock puppets to kill.

The days and nights wear on. Not even the hardest
Heart kept the ocean from its eyes as we soaped down the seals
And otters most of whom died in our arms...

One survivor that day—a blue heron oil-blind
In one eye—so frightened by what no one understands
It reached for us first—it's neck a snake around my wrist—head on my
Raingear—and though this sleight bird weighed only a few
Pounds when it lifted into the sky I knew I'd never
Carry anything so heavy in my life again.

Myrrh

The woman was banished
To the deep woods where she gave birth
Squatting beneath flowering hawthorn
To her daughter who slipped
Out on the earth among
Last seasons' dead leaves and acorns—
Just another sunlit seed.

The mother cleaned this child
With her tongue then brought her
Close to her heart to feed—

The trees remember this.
The sky looking through the trees
Sees everything and forgives
Our blundering down dark roads
Between two fatal lights.

To say more about this
I must visit the collective library
To check out the book
I am afraid to read. Surely
You are braver than I am
Since I believe though it's
Unsigned you authored it.

Mission Drift

On the river pieces of a corduroy
Road broken apart by hurricanes
Float slowly toward the Gulf of Mexico—
As the storm surge lessens gulls feast
Without fear atop the drowned.

A beaver trapped between
The bent girders of a steel bridge
Looks up at the golden sun through the brown river—
Thinks of nothing—regrets nothing—loves
Nothing—leaves nothing behind but its body
Found weeks later by children
Fishing for dinner in a green canal.

This is the story of how light gets
Turned off and how light turns back on—
Ours is the story of all that
Happens in between.

Sidewalk Surfing

Neighbor girl is my best friend—our houses
Close enough to wave through bedroom windows
When sent to our rooms for coming home dirty
From the hot rain after playing tag until there's no light
Left in this enormous world and we didn't care
Who yelled at us for being kids.

She showed me pictures in a magazine
About teens in California doing this strange thing
Called skateboarding so we stole screws
And 2x4s from dads—took the wheels
Off our roller skates and made the first
Skateboard in the neighborhood—it was 1961.

Man did we take some falls. Not
A clue what to do when that thing sped up—
Hit a big crack and the wheels fell off but
Sometimes it was perfect—speed and balance
And joy alive in the scars I carry today—

But that was on another planet
In another dimension when a boy
And a girl could sweat over a tool
Together—reinventing the wheel
With total focus—two becoming one—
Hands sharing the weight—cheeks
Touching and hair entangled—
Sweat dripping on the results—

Four hands—two bodies—one purpose—
Never an idea one of us was better or worth more
Than the other —bending to the task—
The rest of our days the reward.

Brevity's Rainbow

When it seems childhood is over—
When leaves fall and suspicions once
Hidden by foliage dangle without conviction
From skeletal limbs I believe in renewal—
Every year new storefronts appear with new owners
Taking down old calendars to start bonfires
With dead leaves—ice is cracking up north—
Growing old is a river in flood stage altering the land
As it runs to sea—or-an endangered jungle
Where moonlight spoon-feeds pale orchids.

One day the green fuse sputters—
The tree remains leafless all summer—wind picks
Its bark. Branches snap like rifles
In a veteran's troubled dream.

This is the departing—each thing lactating
Its precious goodbye—planets, insects, men and women
Living stories of a verdant origin where life begins
In salt ponds heated by the sun—a soul at the edge
Of the body waiting for brevity's rainbow to begin—
Sunset a requiem for the gods that die when we do.

Least of Us

Grandfather believed rain
Gathers in basins where angels
Clean their wings before entering
The sacristy of mortal form to retrieve
The red scarf death leaves behind.

We'd find him at sunrise after a storm drinking
From birdbaths or puddles—happy to drown
In the holiness of the everyday everywhere—

Of course grandfather was committed
To an asylum by the authorities though they
Willingly enough bought his bottled rain
Said to restore antiquarian glands.

Rest in peace grandfather among the wild
Wolves whispering lonely warnings into a snowy light

Where real heroes discover a previously
Unknow garden made from vowels inside a battle cry
That fibrillates an ancient spirit back
To life—I hear grandfather howling—he's out there
Agreeably listening to flowers.

Minor Chords

The cafe table is covered in wax paper
With a small pot of violets in the center.
There is a candle in a wine bottle the waiter
Will light when it's dark—

Beyond the white wall etched
With faded slogans by patriots
Whose mothers place flowers
Each anniversary of their death
A rust-colored river picks up
Speed before leaving town.

I watch children performing in a blue
Pavilion across the water—some laughing but some
Are sobbing because they forgot their lines—

We are all parents when a child cries.

Snow Forts

In Virginia in 1956
It started snowing one January
And didn't stop for 2 weeks.

I made so much money shoveling walks and driveways
That I bought a transistor radio just to hear my friend
The witch doctor tell me what to do but when I discovered
Chuck Berry my world changed forever.

Roger and I and Suzie hand-scooped holes
In the drifts until we burrowed down into hazy
Pockets of sparkling blue light I'd later
Associate with neon signs in cowboy bars.

We'd turn that radio full blast
Deep in our snow cave—the houses
And the world of parents and made-up
Rules gone while the heat from Buddy Holly's
Stratocaster made the ceiling melt—

Thank you winter for places to hide—for brothers
And sisters and Rock and Roll.

Archives

The practice seems easy—live through
Each moment into the next causing the least
Injury to the self or others while maintaining
A semblance of balance on the high wire
Strung between ebullience and despair.

There are cracks in the foundation—we hear
Them as distant gunshots in shopping malls—
Or maybe it's the voice of a kidnapped sister falling
To pieces on a telephone—maybe it's the national
Anthem that elevates to a degree of reverence
The pennies in a wishing well.

I finish my diary entry for today—[I've seen enough]—
Soak it with gasoline—throw a match on it—fly away
Ladybird—your house is on fire—your children
Are calling—it's time for you to go home.

Acts of Kindness

I walked the blackened cobbles where chariots
Once brought emperors through the streets to the senate
To legislate justice with bejeweled daggers
To my apartment at the top of the tower—up the worn
Stairs so uneven I've tripped on them coming back
With an armful of books—I enter my room—it's never locked
And find Death in my chair crying as it reads my poems
Many of which it inspired—I massage her shoulders—
Offer a soft rag to wipe her eyes—beneath my fingers I
Feel how little flesh there is and yet confess to erotic
Thoughts—I put water on the burner for tea we
Share without a word—I hate my job she says—we
All do I say—but not today she says—you've other poems
To write—then—finishing the tea—she tears this poem
From my book and I sign it—she kisses me—
Her lips are ripe mangoes—her eyes are an ocean
Taken from a tidal wave—glides out the window
Back into the world where someone is sleeping—
Driving a car—loading a gun—opening a door—as
Unprepared as I am to say goodbye.

Street Wedding

Dare to do as you're guided the sage tells the young
Monk who drinks from the forbidden spring at the foot
Of denial then returns to the world appearing
To gurus and car salesmen as a poorly aimed
Cannonball shot from karma.

Somewhere a person is walking behind an ass cart—
A load of seed to distribute—the fertilizer underfoot—

My ignorance is a book no library is big enough
To hold—the last eagle marooned above the city
Looks down at stragglers pouring from a jazz joint—it's
Closing time all over the world—the streets are formidable
With the dying echoes of horns—a bankrupt ghost
Picks the pockets of drunk entrepreneurs—

In solidarity with the desperate I'm dragged behind a tank
Out of the cellar where old testimonials are stacked atop
Cabbages—it's lovely to receive the gift of distance by stepping
Closer to the problem in this case the cop directing traffic
With a weathervane—the cabbages sing praises in Aramaic
So loudly I can't hear you scream—when everyone looks away
We look at each other and say—I do.

Enough

This perfect sunrise followed
Immediately by this perfect sunset
Instills an overwhelming climb a tree feeling
As we help elderly flowers find the light
And this is almost enough.

The peace of mind that comes
To the farmer baling dry hay in fields
Where the rain held off is close but
Not quite enough.

The new foal asleep in the shade
Of its mother as the autumn sun gently dries it
Is almost in itself sufficient.

Your hand inside the same glove
With mine—the animal tracks clairvoyants
Make in the air foretelling my longing
To live another day to see you smile—
This is enough.

Monsters

The little boy was 9 and the oldest
Of 4 brothers so it was okay he babysat
Them while his parents played cards next door
Fifty feet away with a neighbor
Couple that had no children.

The brothers were at the kitchen chewing crayons
Or drawing stick figures— the little boy was coloring
A tiger—his favorite animal—he had decals
On his schoolbag and a tiger t-shirt and a tiger
Lunchbox—his nickname was Tiger.

Outside the screen door came a growling
Sound that got louder—tigers the boy thought as his brothers
Cried and hid under the table—

The little boy didn't cry or hide—he grabbed
A big knife from the kitchen counter then ran to the door
As the growling got so loud he thought his heart
Would stop—the door flew open—a shadow burst in—
The boy didn't run away—he defended
His brothers and his home—he ran at the tiger
And slashed it with the big knife.
It was his father—come over to
Check on the boys and scare them a little.

When his father came back from the hospital with his arm bandaged—
A red spot forming under the gauze—he told everyone
To stop yelling at the little boy—he did his job—he was
The man of the house when everyone was gone.

The little boy tore up all his coloring books
And peeled tiger decals from his bike.

He still loves tigers.
But he doesn't believe there's any left—
I killed the last one.

Biome

A little girl in faded striped
Overalls is piling freshly cut grass
Near a culvert because the city
Just mowed it all down— depriving the spring
Peepers of their habitat—she's
Diligently piling up the grass then
Using a watering can to dampen it
In layers—the ditch is deep enough
And the sun seasonal enough that no
Light will completely dry it out—
She's not my daughter—in fact
She's not real—if anything she's the source
Of the woman I am now stirring
An empty pot with an invisible
Spoon before inviting all my
Ghosts to dinner.

Bonsai Angel

For not the first time
I wake up still drunk in the pre-dawn
Dark outside my favorite bar
Curled around a streetlamp illuminating
The road to oblivion while hosting
A silent wake for a former life where
I got these scars without honor.

I shake the kaleidoscope—memories
Of jukebox rhymes—short tempers and wet
Kisses like pixie dust on a wedding coat—older
Memories of slit trenches and heavy packs—
The world too much to carry—I lean against the lamp—
Dislodge a raucous belch startling pigeons—
Dodge citizens embellishing a fiction—
No small comfort to be found.

I finger-comb my way down the sidewalk
Then stagger back into the night
That just ended.

Insomnia

A poet in a puddle on the floor at midnight
In a closed museum struggling to make sense
Of the Great Auk a note describes as stuffed with wadding
By lantern light alongside a river of groaning
Ice by scientists—is this a poem or a mental breakdown—

Rising from my own derivatives I meditate on rubber
Bands pulled equally in all directions—the yellow light
Is a warning to slow down but it's too late—the world drove
Past the point of no return—traffic accelerates—when the light
Turns red—a nation hangs out a foreclosure sign—
I see the soot on the wrist of a grandmother pulled
Up the chimney by storks—someone ran the red light—
The collision is spectacular—no one seems hurt but everyone
Is dead except the last romantic who applies
The jaws of life to save Ann Bolyn's cleavage.

Not my cup of tea says the chimpanzee near the top
Branches of the evolutionary tree—it's enough
To escape the zoologists in this poem—god
I wish sleep would come so I could wake up.

My grandmother carried spoons of rainwater
To make a lagoon to provide a place for the moon
To rest—I'm still the infant in her kitchen—the radio
Plays a song about cottonwoods—I drool
Mashed peas on my bib—grandfather wipes my face—
I hear my husband and a stranger picked up
Hitchhiking dispute the ownership of sunset
Over black coffee outside a tiny bistro in Athens—
We're jazzed but it's not the coffee—it's the smell
Of marjoram and garlic coming from the lamb
Rotating above the hot coals across the street—night
Comes among us to write another page in the book
The stars hope it won't finish—I'm tired of refereeing
Fights between the old gods that chew petunias
Then piddle on the floor and blame the cat—

The marriage bed is an instrument playing loud music
In the key of kiss my ass—I toss and turn—get up
To spray paint graffiti on the bridge between my eyeballs—
Dance around the empty bed to Param singing That Girl—
The paint on the bridge is dry enough to touch—

I have no memory of what just went down—first light lands
Like an astronaut on the moon with only a semaphore to keep in touch
With her conscience—the poet confesses to the friars
In the toaster the poem is ready but the marmalade is rancid—
Never mind says the muse sipping black coffee—what's
Bad for you is equally medicine—through the blinds
The sun comes calling—I hope I never sleep again.

Requiem for Sylvia

Happiness drains from your smile
When the yellow finch hits the window on a beautiful
Spring day—throwing itself through all that
Light filled with an arial joy—its song
Half-finished when it dies—

I place her—a female by its drab
Feathers—in the palm of my hand while
You dig the grave—deep down into the black earth
Beneath the blue cypress and as we walk away
You pick up the bird's song—at first so low
I mistake it for the Ave Maria annuals
Whisper as winter comes—but no—

It's you—in the voice of women everywhere—
Finishing the song of the finch as you fly away.

Rough Grace

After a year welding miles of pipe
In Prudhoe Bay I went south by southwest
To Nome to spend the winter
In a concrete block room attached
To a hangar in the small airport—we
Listened to the radio talk about bear
Sightings above the roar of the furnace
While drinking boiled coffee with whiskey
To start the day then out on the line
Schnapps to keep the cold away.

I worked trap lines with an old Yupik fiddler
With no teeth who kept his rosin mixed with snuff
In a bag around his neck—he owned a seven-dog sled
We mushed into the iced-over world out
Where human footprints end and the stink of mink
On cold steel—the locking sound of a trap—
Sheered bones of fisher pushing through fur blew
Across the silent bloody snow while over it all
The suffering sky struggled in salt ponds.

I was young—needed to feel the cruelty of the world
So later I could live in it without going crazy—
So I could watch children pulled from mothers
At borders by monsters—see nooses hung from live oak
Trees—watch tenderness forfeited to the bottom line
And still breathe because I followed the tallyman's
Tracks to a corpse through the frozen trees.

One morning the old fiddler went to check the traps—
I stayed behind with a couple frostbit toes he offered
To take off with his skinning knife—as a favor
You understand—he never came back.

I went out the next morning following his tracks
To a rattling stand of bony willows—found him curled up dead—
Caught in the trap by his bow hand—surrounded
By piss markers and partially eaten by wolves.

I caught a Twin Otter to Dillingham
Then back home to the lake where I sat alone
In my cabin thinking of karma—writing bad poems
While planning the next desperate interlude—I guess you
Could say I was waiting for Easter—for the stone to move—
For the wolves that finally found me.

Fathers

I perch at the edge of a glimpse
Overlooking fields of purple
Heather mitered by wind
Into one another in a ceaseless
Dance of bondage to purpose
And beauty and the gray
Fumes seeping out of the tin
Mines of Cornwall—
Moist openings in the earth
Rimed with smoke spread
Across the lumpen hills
That need only an old briar
Pipe to remind the child
Of father asleep in a chair—
Pipe in hand——smoke in the room—
Smoke in the earth—our
Bodies—the smell of whiskey
And smelter grit in his hair.

Even exhausted—so near to death
He was never unkind.

I take the pipe
From his hand—say a child's
Prayer for tomorrow—puff
Once on the pipe—place heather
My favorite agate and one drab
Wing feather on his lap.
He sleeps like ore.

Does he dream of blocked exits
Inside old mines—his hands twitch—maybe
Lighting his pipe underground—maybe
God's finger on his wrist—counting pulses—

Only the moon with its dark side
Hidden understands how he survived—assaulted—
Tilted—jilted—adrift—down there alone—sharing
The little light he had to show
A lost child the way home.

God's Morgue

Follow the strings—impossible it seems to believe
In normal—the miracles we see are ordinary in other worlds—
Infinity is a big place—eventually everything happens—
An elderly monkey will type flawlessly the dead sea
Scrolls—the soldier surrendered her leg to dance with a gun—
She waits on the hill overlooking the farmhouse
For the lights to go out at which point—rifle abandoned—shoe
In hand—she mothers the tiny, penned piglets—

In the freezing storage room through a steamed
Window god looks over the black bags—each one with a foot
Sticking out with a tag on it—date of death—no name—god didn't
Name the angels—we did— most are here though a few escaped
He thinks—on the run—disguised as prairie dogs
Or wasps—god is at home in this place of no names—-
His cleaver drags the floor making a sound that reminds
Him of one of his heroes freed briefly in a Poe story—
God's eyes are red—he coughs liquid doves—it's almost time—

He lays down on the bed he made—wraps a tag around
His toe—writes the time—today—falls asleep
Trying to remember his name.

Migration

The adults and children are shadows in the house—
They sing new songs mimicking the ancient stories
Of lost crops in blackened fields and cradles—migrating
Faces lifted to the blistering sun—how it came to be
We are here—next door an elderly woman recites poetry
She writes while the house sleeps—in the courtyard shared
By three houses the red stones turn white from sunlight
But in one corner under an orange tree the stones are brown
From centuries of rotting fruit—that's how long
We've been here—the woman's poems remember the day
Her lips were forced to kiss a soldier's gun.

***

In the crown of evening sky a bombing run begins.
The pilot is little more than a child playing a video game
In which nothing is real but the numb dumb hand is deadly—
The courtyard grows silent—the woman carries her shadow—
Waiting—the dog's tail is wrapped around its head so it's slow
To notice the sound of bees in the Faqqu'a iris becoming the hum
Of slowing rotors—both pollinators likely crossed the Negev.
The drone passes over the white stones—the sun
Gets hotter—this time we are spared.

***

In a world of hidden cameras and spectators
That lie about what they see miracles still happen—
The shy boys are afraid to talk to girls—the girls
Are plainly ambivalent and so wait for timidity and
Kindness to combine with desire to paint a fresco a woman
Might inhabit—the boys toot like hoopoes in the ripe
Oranges—their thin beaks finding inside the tough skin
Something sweet elated to be found—fathers smoke
With fathers on chairs made unstable by the stones
Of the courtyard—time is shifting—mothers watch out windows—
Where have the messengers of faith gone.

***

At the edge of belief a cataract of stones buzz
The way rumors spread through telephone lines—
Is it time to stop dancing just because the music ended—
To admit to a weariness for which the cure
Is not sleep but action—the hoopoes ebb and flow
Their entire lives between shifting horizons—why ask
If they are satisfied—they alone choose where to land
And now they've flown—-the iris petals begin underground then
Explode when struck by a light so foreign they cry out
In shades of violet—anther—stem and pollen—swelling
Despite the thickened air—the entreaties—-words
Hammered into prayer—into monsters and heroes
Fighting in a slant of dust— the music now footsteps
Dragging a dimming light between bodies.

***

What is passed on is knowledge not wisdom—
One turns into the other through hard work—what
Comes easy can't be trusted—the bird can't tell her egg
How to fly—my mother speaks loudly when no one
Is around—she whispers to me now—look closely my love—
We are the windows in the target through which
Light escapes before it's turned off—I dared to have babies—
Stone by stone our house is rebuilt—rejoice—we are here—
The oranges are ripe again—the hoopoes have
Come back through air nobody owns—I am

Asking you to believe they were never gone—
They are always here—those messengers of faith
Drinking sweetness from our glorious garden.

Few Will Know

We spent late autumn days
Drying rosemary and sage for winter stews—
Canning vegetables on the wood stove
In the summer kitchen with the steam
Rising from the big enamel
Kettle into our sweaty faces—the quart
Jars on the sideboard snapping
As they seal—a chill in the air—
Swallows taking off from under eaves—
Hornets busy chewing trees
Into paper houses and the horses
Restless in the pasture—gathered
At the fence and as one animal
Looking westward—we see what they see
And seal the windows—light fires—
Shovel snow—learn how to love
When the blood to the heart grows slow—
When it's time to go back outside
The horses let us know.

About the Author

Gary Lemons has been writing poetry since 1965. He attended Breadloaf Writers Conference in 1971 and 1972 and graduated from the Undergraduate Poetry Workshop at the U. of Iowa in 1975. He has studied with some of the great poets of his and any generation including Norman Dubie, Maxine Kumin, William Stafford, John Berryman, Diane Wakowski and Donald Justice. None of whom are to blame for what he made of their guidance. He has published 9 books of poetry including the Snake Quartet. His 10th book is scheduled for release in Spring of 2026 with Moon Tide Press. Of the many things he's done to support his writing he's most grateful for the time spent reforesting clearcuts in the PNW where he planted over 400,000 trees. He lives in Port Townsend, Wa between the sea and the mountains with his life partner Nöle Giulini to whom this and all his books are dedicated.

Acknowledgements

Love and gratitude to my parents
And teachers—visible, as well as invisible—

In Particular

Kate Gale
Jenny Van West
Amirah Al Wassif
Hanno Giulini
Eric Morago
Norman Dubie
Clint Willis
Sharon Doubiago
Shabnam Merchandi
Alicia Mathias
Erich Schiffmann
John Huey
Jo Morton
W. Nick Hill
Mark Cull
Adrianne Kalfopoulou
Dirk Nelson
Anne Jablonski
Kelly Lee
Alexis Rhone-Fancher
Sam Hamill

Also Available from Moon Tide Press

Frozen Fawn, Ally McGregor (2026)
The Ground Never Lets Go, Liz Marlow (2026)
Afterburn, Rebecca Evans (2026)
Not So Fast, Sarah McMahon (2026)
The Elephant of Surprise, Charles Harper Webb (2026)
Outliving Michael, Steven Reigns (2025)
Prayers With a Side of Cash, Kathleen Florence (2025)
Somewhere, a Playground, Rich Ferguson (2025)
The Tautology of Water, Giovanni Boskovich (2025)
Take Care, Mark Danowsky (2025)
Dilapitatia, Kelly Gray (2025)
Reluctant Prophets, J.D. Isip (2025)
Enormous Blue Umbrella, Donna Hilbert (2025)
Sky Leaning Toward Winter, Terri Niccum (2024)
Living the Sundown: A Caregiving Memoir, G. Murray Thomas (2024)
Figure Study, Kathryn de Lancellotti (2024)
Suffer for This: Love, Sex, Marriage, & Rock 'N' Roll, Victor D. Infante (2024)
What Blooms in the Dark, Emily J. Mundy (2024)
Fable, Bryn Wickerd (2024)
Diamond Bars 2, David A. Romero (2024)
Safe Handling, Rebecca Evans (2024)
More Jerkumstances: New & Selected Poems, Barbara Eknoian (2024)
Dissection Day, Ally McGregor (2023)
He's a Color Until He's Not, Christian Hanz Lozada (2023)
The Language of Fractions, Nicelle Davis (2023)
Paradise Anonymous, Oriana Ivy (2023)
Now You Are a Missing Person, Susan Hayden (2023)
Maze Mouth, Brian Sonia-Wallace (2023)
Tangled by Blood, Rebecca Evans (2023)
Another Way of Loving Death, Jeremy Ra (2023)
Kissing the Wound, J.D. Isip (2023)
Feed It to the River, Terhi K. Cherry (2022)

Beat Not Beat: An Anthology of California Poets Screwing on the Beat and Post-Beat Tradition (2022)
When There Are Nine: Poems Celebrating the Life and Achievements of Ruth Bader Ginsburg (2022)
The Knife Thrower's Daughter, Terri Niccum (2022)
2 Revere Place, Aruni Wijesinghe (2022)
Here Go the Knives, Kelsey Bryan-Zwick (2022)
Trumpets in the Sky, Jerry Garcia (2022)
Threnody, Donna Hilbert (2022)
A Burning Lake of Paper Suns, Ellen Webre (2021)
Instructions for an Animal Body, Kelly Gray (2021)
*Head *V* Heart: New & Selected Poems*, Rob Sturma (2021)
Sh!t Men Say to Me: A Poetry Anthology in Response to Toxic Masculinity (2021)
Flower Grand First, Gustavo Hernandez (2021)
Everything is Radiant Between the Hates, Rich Ferguson (2020)
When the Pain Starts: Poetry as Sequential Art, Alan Passman (2020)
This Place Could Be Haunted If I Didn't Believe in Love, Lincoln McElwee (2020)
Impossible Thirst, Kathryn de Lancellotti (2020)
Lullabies for End Times, Jennifer Bradpiece (2020)
Crabgrass World, Robin Axworthy (2020)
Contortionist Tongue, Dania Ayah Alkhouli (2020)
The only thing that makes sense is to grow, Scott Ferry (2020)
Dead Letter Box, Terri Niccum (2019)
Tea and Subtitles: Selected Poems 1999-2019, Michael Miller (2019)
At the Table of the Unknown, Alexandra Umlas (2019)
The Book of Rabbits, Vince Trimboli (2019)
Everything I Write Is a Love Song to the World, David McIntire (2019)
Letters to the Leader, HanaLena Fennel (2019)
Darwin's Garden, Lee Rossi (2019)
Dark Ink: A Poetry Anthology Inspired by Horror (2018)
Drop and Dazzle, Peggy Dobreer (2018)
Junkie Wife, Alexis Rhone Fancher (2018)
The Moon, My Lover, My Mother, & the Dog, Daniel McGinn (2018)

Lullaby of Teeth: An Anthology of Southern California Poetry (2017)
Angels in Seven, Michael Miller (2016)
A Likely Story, Robbi Nester (2014)
Embers on the Stairs, Ruth Bavetta (2014)
The Green of Sunset, John Brantingham (2013)
The Savagery of Bone, Timothy Matthew Perez (2013)
The Silence of Doorways, Sharon Venezio (2013)
Cosmos: An Anthology of Southern California Poetry (2012)
Straws and Shadows, Irena Praitis (2012)
In the Lake of Your Bones, Peggy Dobreer (2012)
I Was Building Up to Something, Susan Davis (2011)
Hopeless Cases, Michael Kramer (2011)
One World, Gail Newman (2011)
What We Ache For, Eric Morago (2010)
Now and Then, Lee Mallory (2009)
Pop Art: An Anthology of Southern California Poetry (2009)
In the Heaven of Never Before, Carine Topal (2008)
A Wild Region, Kate Buckley (2008)
Carving in Bone: An Anthology of Orange County Poetry (2007)
Kindness from a Dark God, Ben Trigg (2007)
A Thin Strand of Lights, Ricki Mandeville (2006)
Sleepyhead Assassins, Mindy Nettifee (2006)
Tide Pools: An Anthology of Orange County Poetry (2006)
Lost American Nights: Lyrics & Poems, Michael Ubaldini (2006)

Patrons

Moon Tide Press would like to thank the following people for their support in helping publish the finest poetry from the Southern California region. To sign up as a patron, visit www.moontidepress.com or send an email to publisher@moontidepress.com.

Anonymous
Robin Axworthy
Conner Brenner
Nicole Connolly
Bill Cushing
Susan Davis
Kristen Baum DeBeasi
Peggy Dobreer
Kate Gale
Dennis Gowans
Alexis Rhone Fancher
HanaLena Fennel
Half Off Books & Brad T. Cox
Donna Hilbert
Jim & Vicky Hoggatt
Michael Kramer
Ron Koertge & Bianca Richards
Gary Jacobelly
Ray & Christi Lacoste
Jeffery Lewis
Zachary & Tammy Locklin
Lincoln McElwee
David McIntire
José Enrique Medina
Michael Miller & Rachanee Srisavasdi
Michelle & Robert Miller
Ronny & Richard Morago
Terri Niccum
Andrew November
Jeremy Ra
Luke & Mia Salazar
Jennifer Smith
Roger Sponder
Andrew Turner
Rex Wilder
Mariano Zaro
Wes Bryan Zwick

www.ingramcontent.com/pod-product-compliance
Lightning Source LLC
LaVergne TN
LVHW051013080826
845145LV00009B/2593

* 9 7 8 1 9 5 7 7 9 9 5 1 3 *